GERM___ .

VEGETARIAN

COOKBOOK

OLIVE LINDEN

CONTENTS

OBATZDA (BAVARIAN CHEESE SPREAD)

Servings: 4

Ingredients:

- 200g (7 oz) Camembert cheese, ripe
- 50g (1.75 oz) cream cheese
- 50g (1.75 oz) unsalted butter, softened
- 1 small onion, finely chopped
- 1 tsp sweet paprika
- ½ tsp caraway seeds (optional)
- Salt and black pepper, to taste
- 1-2 tbsp beer (optional, for authenticity)
- Chives, chopped (for garnish)

Instructions:

1. In a bowl, mash the Camembert with a fork until smooth.
2. Add the cream cheese and softened butter, mixing well.
3. Stir in the chopped onion, paprika, caraway seeds (if using), salt, and black pepper.
4. If using, add beer a little at a time to get a smooth, spreadable consistency.
5. Let it sit in the fridge for at least 30 minutes to allow the flavors to meld.
6. Garnish with chopped chives and serve with pretzels or rye bread.

PRETZELS WITH MUSTARD DIP

Servings: 6 Pretzels

Ingredients for Pretzels:

- 500g (4 cups) all-purpose flour
- 1 packet (7g / 2 ¼ tsp) dry yeast
- 1 tsp salt
- 1 tsp sugar
- 300ml (1 ¼ cups) warm water
- 2 tbsp unsalted butter, melted
- 3 tbsp baking soda (for boiling)
- Coarse salt (for topping)

Ingredients for Mustard Dip:

- 3 tbsp Dijon mustard
- 2 tbsp whole grain mustard
- 2 tbsp honey (or maple syrup for vegan option)
- 2 tbsp sour cream or Greek yogurt
- ½ tsp apple cider vinegar
- Black pepper, to taste

Instructions:

Making the Pretzels:

1. In a bowl, mix warm water, sugar, and yeast. Let sit for 5 minutes until frothy.
2. Add flour, salt, and melted butter. Knead into a smooth dough (about 8-10 minutes).
3. Cover and let rise in a warm place for 1 hour until doubled in size.

4. Preheat oven to 220°C (425°F). Line a baking sheet with parchment paper.
5. Divide dough into 6 equal pieces. Roll each into a long rope (about 50 cm / 20 inches) and shape into a pretzel.
6. Bring a pot of water to a boil, add baking soda, then briefly dip each pretzel (about 30 seconds).
7. Place pretzels on the baking sheet, sprinkle with coarse salt, and bake for 12-15 minutes until golden brown.

Making the Mustard Dip:

8. In a small bowl, mix Dijon mustard, whole grain mustard, honey, sour cream, vinegar, and black pepper. Stir well.
9. Serve alongside warm pretzels.

KARTOFFELPUFFER (POTATO PANCAKES) WITH APPLESAUCE

Servings: 4 (Makes about 8 pancakes)

Ingredients for Kartoffelpuffer:

- 4 medium potatoes, peeled and grated
- 1 small onion, grated
- 1 egg (or flax egg for vegan option)
- 2 tbsp all-purpose flour
- ½ tsp salt
- ¼ tsp black pepper
- ¼ tsp nutmeg (optional)
- Vegetable oil, for frying

Ingredients for Applesauce:

- 3 apples, peeled, cored, and chopped
- 2 tbsp water
- 1 tbsp sugar (optional)
- ½ tsp cinnamon (optional)

Instructions:

Make the Applesauce:

1. In a small saucepan, add chopped apples and water.
2. Cover and cook over medium heat for 10-15 minutes until soft.
3. Mash with a fork or blend for a smoother texture. Add sugar and cinnamon, if desired. Set aside.

Make the Potato Pancakes:

4. Place grated potatoes and onion in a clean kitchen towel and squeeze out excess liquid.
5. In a bowl, mix potatoes, onion, egg, flour, salt, pepper, and nutmeg.
6. Heat oil in a frying pan over medium heat.
7. Drop spoonfuls of the potato mixture into the pan, flattening them slightly.
8. Fry for 3-4 minutes per side until golden brown and crispy.
9. Drain on paper towels.

FLAMMKUCHEN (ALSATIAN-STYLE FLATBREAD)

Servings: 4 (Makes 2 Flatbreads)

Ingredients for the Dough:

- 250g (2 cups) all-purpose flour
- ½ tsp salt
- 2 tbsp olive oil
- 120ml (½ cup) water

Ingredients for the Topping:

- 150g (⅔ cup) crème fraîche or sour cream (use plant-based alternative for vegan)
- 1 small onion, thinly sliced
- 100g (3.5 oz) mushrooms, thinly sliced
- ½ tsp salt
- ¼ tsp black pepper
- ½ tsp nutmeg (optional)
- 1 tbsp chives or green onions, chopped (for garnish)

Instructions:

1. **Make the Dough:**
   - In a bowl, mix flour and salt.
   - Add olive oil and water, kneading into a smooth dough. Let rest for 15 minutes.
2. **Prepare the Toppings:**
   - Mix crème fraîche with salt, pepper, and nutmeg.
   - Slice onions and mushrooms thinly.
3. **Assemble the Flammkuchen:**
   - Preheat oven to 250°C (480°F) and place a baking sheet or pizza stone inside.

- o Divide dough into two portions and roll out very thin.
- o Spread crème fraîche mixture over the dough.
- o Top with onions and mushrooms.

4. **Bake:**
   - o Transfer to the hot baking sheet and bake for 8-10 minutes, until crispy and golden.

5. **Garnish & Serve:**
   - o Sprinkle with fresh chives or green onions and serve immediately.

GERMAN VEGETARIAN COOKBOOK

KOHLRABI CARPACCIO WITH WALNUTS & PARMESAN

Servings: 2-3

Ingredients:

- 1 medium kohlrabi, peeled and thinly sliced
- 30g (¼ cup) walnuts, chopped
- 30g (¼ cup) Parmesan cheese, shaved (use vegan Parmesan if needed)
- 2 tbsp olive oil
- 1 tbsp lemon juice
- 1 tsp honey or maple syrup (for vegan option)
- ½ tsp Dijon mustard
- Salt and black pepper, to taste
- Fresh parsley or arugula, for garnish

Instructions:

1. **Prepare the Kohlrabi:**
   - Peel the kohlrabi and slice it very thinly (use a mandoline if available). Arrange the slices on a serving plate.
2. **Make the Dressing:**
   - In a small bowl, whisk together olive oil, lemon juice, honey (or maple syrup), Dijon mustard, salt, and pepper.
3. **Assemble the Dish:**
   - Drizzle the dressing over the sliced kohlrabi.
   - Sprinkle with chopped walnuts and shaved Parmesan.
4. **Garnish & Serve:**
   - Top with fresh parsley or arugula for extra color and freshness.

ROTE BETE CARPACCIO (BEET CARPACCIO)

Servings: 2-3

Ingredients:

- 2 medium beets, cooked and peeled
- 30g (¼ cup) walnuts or hazelnuts, chopped
- 30g (¼ cup) goat cheese or feta, crumbled (use plant-based cheese if needed)
- 1 tbsp olive oil
- 1 tbsp balsamic vinegar
- 1 tsp honey or maple syrup (for vegan option)
- ½ tsp Dijon mustard
- Salt and black pepper, to taste
- Fresh arugula or microgreens, for garnish

Instructions:

1. **Prepare the Beets:**
   - Thinly slice the cooked and peeled beets using a sharp knife or mandoline. Arrange the slices on a plate in a single layer.
2. **Make the Dressing:**
   - In a small bowl, whisk together olive oil, balsamic vinegar, honey (or maple syrup), Dijon mustard, salt, and pepper.
3. **Assemble the Carpaccio:**
   - Drizzle the dressing over the sliced beets.
   - Sprinkle with chopped nuts and crumbled cheese.
4. **Garnish & Serve:**
   - Top with fresh arugula or microgreens for added freshness.

ZWIEBELKUCHEN (ONION TART)

Servings: 6-8

Ingredients for the Dough:

- 250g (2 cups) all-purpose flour
- ½ tsp salt
- 1 tsp sugar
- 1 packet (7g / 2 ¼ tsp) dry yeast
- 125ml (½ cup) warm milk (or plant-based milk)
- 2 tbsp unsalted butter, melted (or olive oil)

Ingredients for the Filling:

- 3 large onions, thinly sliced
- 1 tbsp butter or olive oil
- 200g (¾ cup) sour cream or crème fraîche (use plant-based for vegan)
- 2 eggs (or 2 tbsp cornstarch + 2 tbsp water for vegan option)
- ½ tsp salt
- ¼ tsp black pepper
- ½ tsp caraway seeds (optional)
- 50g (½ cup) grated cheese (Emmental or Gouda, optional)

Instructions:

Prepare the Dough:

1. In a bowl, mix warm milk, sugar, and yeast. Let sit for 5 minutes until frothy.
2. Add flour, salt, and melted butter. Knead into a smooth dough.
3. Cover and let rise for 45-60 minutes until doubled in size.

Prepare the Filling:

4. In a pan, heat butter or oil over medium heat. Add sliced onions and cook until soft and translucent (about 10 minutes).
5. In a bowl, mix sour cream, eggs, salt, pepper, and caraway seeds. Stir in the sautéed onions.

Assemble & Bake:

6. Preheat oven to 200°C (400°F). Roll out the dough and press it into a greased tart pan.
7. Pour the onion mixture over the dough, spreading it evenly. Sprinkle cheese on top if using.
8. Bake for 30-35 minutes until golden brown.
9. Let cool slightly, then slice and serve warm.

KARTOFFELSUPPE (CREAMY GERMAN POTATO SOUP)

Servings: 4

Ingredients:

- 500g (1 lb) potatoes, peeled and diced
- 1 small onion, chopped
- 1 carrot, chopped
- 1 leek, sliced
- 1 clove garlic, minced
- 1 tbsp butter or oil
- 750ml (3 cups) vegetable broth
- 125ml (½ cup) heavy cream or plant-based cream
- ½ tsp salt
- ¼ tsp black pepper

- ½ tsp marjoram (optional)
- Fresh chives or parsley, chopped (for garnish)

Instructions:

1. **Sauté the Vegetables:**
    - Heat butter or oil in a pot over medium heat.
    - Add onions, leeks, carrots, and garlic. Sauté for 3-4 minutes until softened.
2. **Cook the Potatoes:**
    - Add diced potatoes and pour in the vegetable broth.
    - Bring to a boil, then reduce heat and simmer for 20 minutes until potatoes are soft.
3. **Blend the Soup:**
    - Use an immersion blender to blend the soup until creamy (or leave it chunky if preferred).
4. **Finish & Season:**
    - Stir in cream, salt, pepper, and marjoram. Simmer for 2 more minutes.
5. **Serve:**
    - Garnish with fresh chives or parsley and serve warm with crusty bread.

LAUCHSUPPE (LEEK SOUP)

Servings: 4

Ingredients:

- 3 large leeks, cleaned and sliced
- 1 small onion, chopped
- 1 tbsp butter or olive oil
- 750ml (3 cups) vegetable broth
- 250ml (1 cup) heavy cream or plant-based cream
- 2 medium potatoes, peeled and diced (optional, for a thicker soup)
- ½ tsp salt
- ¼ tsp black pepper
- ½ tsp nutmeg (optional)
- Fresh chives or parsley, chopped (for garnish)

Instructions:

1. **Sauté the Vegetables:**
   o Heat butter or oil in a pot over medium heat.
   o Add onions and leeks, sautéing for 5 minutes until soft.
2. **Simmer the Soup:**
   o Add potatoes (if using) and pour in the vegetable broth.
   o Bring to a boil, then reduce heat and let simmer for 15-20 minutes until potatoes are tender.
3. **Blend & Finish:**
   o Use an immersion blender to blend the soup until smooth (or leave it slightly chunky if preferred).
   o Stir in cream, salt, pepper, and nutmeg. Simmer for 2 more minutes.
4. **Serve:**
   o Garnish with fresh chives or parsley and serve warm.

ERBSENSUPPE (GERMAN SPLIT PEA SOUP)

Servings: 4-6

Ingredients:

- 250g (1 ¼ cups) dried split peas, rinsed
- 1 small onion, chopped
- 1 carrot, diced
- 1 leek, sliced
- 1 celery stalk, diced
- 1 clove garlic, minced
- 1 tbsp butter or oil
- 1 liter (4 cups) vegetable broth
- 1 bay leaf
- ½ tsp marjoram (optional)
- ½ tsp salt
- ¼ tsp black pepper
- ½ tsp mustard (optional, for extra flavor)
- 2 medium potatoes, peeled and diced
- Fresh parsley, chopped (for garnish)

Instructions:

1. **Sauté the Vegetables:**
   - Heat butter or oil in a large pot over medium heat.
   - Add onion, garlic, carrot, leek, and celery. Sauté for 5 minutes until softened.
2. **Cook the Split Peas:**
   - Add the rinsed split peas, vegetable broth, bay leaf, marjoram, salt, and pepper.
   - Bring to a boil, then reduce heat and let simmer for 30 minutes.
3. **Add the Potatoes:**

- o Stir in the diced potatoes and cook for another 20-30 minutes until everything is soft.

4. **Blend (Optional) & Finish:**
   - o For a smoother soup, blend part of it with an immersion blender.
   - o Stir in mustard (if using) and adjust seasoning to taste.

5. **Serve:**
   - o Remove bay leaf, garnish with fresh parsley, and serve warm with crusty bread.

BAYERISCHER WURSTSALAT (VEGETARIAN SAUSAGE SALAD)

Servings: 2-3

Ingredients:

- 200g (7 oz) vegetarian or vegan sausage, thinly sliced
- 1 small onion, thinly sliced
- 2 pickles, thinly sliced
- 1 tbsp capers (optional)
- 1 tbsp fresh chives, chopped

Dressing:

- 2 tbsp white wine vinegar
- 1 tbsp vegetable oil
- 1 tsp Dijon mustard
- ½ tsp sugar
- ¼ tsp salt
- ¼ tsp black pepper

Instructions:

1. **Prepare the Ingredients:**
   - Slice the vegetarian sausage, onion, and pickles into thin strips.
2. **Make the Dressing:**
   - In a small bowl, whisk together vinegar, oil, mustard, sugar, salt, and pepper.
3. **Assemble the Salad:**
   - In a mixing bowl, combine sausage, onions, pickles, and capers.
   - Pour the dressing over the salad and toss to coat.

4. **Chill & Serve:**
   o Let the salad sit in the fridge for at least 30 minutes to allow the flavors to meld.
   o Garnish with fresh chives and serve with pretzels or rye bread.

GURKENSALAT (CREAMY CUCUMBER SALAD)

Servings: 4

Ingredients:

- 1 large cucumber, thinly sliced
- ½ small onion, finely chopped (optional)
- 150g (½ cup) sour cream or Greek yogurt (use plant-based for vegan)
- 1 tbsp white vinegar or lemon juice
- 1 tsp sugar
- ½ tsp salt
- ¼ tsp black pepper
- 1 tbsp fresh dill, chopped (or 1 tsp dried dill)

Instructions:

1. **Prepare the Cucumber:**
   - Thinly slice the cucumber using a knife or mandoline.
   - If the cucumber is watery, sprinkle with a little salt and let sit for 10 minutes. Drain excess liquid.
2. **Make the Dressing:**
   - In a bowl, mix sour cream, vinegar, sugar, salt, pepper, and dill.
3. **Assemble the Salad:**
   - Add the sliced cucumber and onions (if using) to the dressing. Toss well to coat.
4. **Chill & Serve:**
   - Let the salad sit in the fridge for at least 15 minutes to allow the flavors to blend.

SAUERKRAUTSALAT (SAUERKRAUT SALAD)

Servings: 4

Ingredients:

- 300g (2 cups) sauerkraut, drained
- ½ small onion, finely chopped
- 1 small apple, grated or finely chopped
- 1 small carrot, grated
- 1 tbsp vegetable oil
- 1 tbsp apple cider vinegar
- 1 tsp sugar or honey (optional)
- ½ tsp caraway seeds (optional)
- Salt and black pepper, to taste
- Fresh parsley, chopped (for garnish)

Instructions:

1. **Prepare the Ingredients:**
   - Drain the sauerkraut and, if it's too sour, rinse it briefly under water and squeeze out excess liquid.
   - Finely chop the onion and apple, and grate the carrot.
2. **Make the Dressing:**
   - In a bowl, whisk together oil, vinegar, sugar (if using), caraway seeds, salt, and black pepper.
3. **Assemble the Salad:**
   - In a mixing bowl, combine the sauerkraut, onion, apple, and carrot.
   - Pour the dressing over and mix well.
4. **Chill & Serve:**
   - Let the salad sit in the fridge for at least 30 minutes to allow the flavors to meld.
   - Garnish with fresh parsley before serving.

ROTE LINSENSUPPE (GERMAN RED LENTIL SOUP)

Servings: 4

Ingredients:

- 200g (1 cup) red lentils, rinsed
- 1 small onion, chopped
- 1 carrot, diced
- 1 clove garlic, minced
- 1 tbsp butter or olive oil
- 750ml (3 cups) vegetable broth
- 1 small potato, diced (optional, for extra creaminess)
- ½ tsp salt
- ¼ tsp black pepper
- ½ tsp paprika
- ½ tsp cumin (optional, for a warm depth of flavor)
- ½ tsp dried marjoram (optional, for a traditional German touch)
- 100ml (⅓ cup) heavy cream or plant-based cream
- Fresh parsley, chopped (for garnish)

Instructions:

1. **Sauté the Vegetables:**
   o Heat butter or oil in a pot over medium heat.
   o Add onions, carrots, and garlic. Sauté for 3-4 minutes until softened.
2. **Cook the Lentils:**
   o Add the rinsed lentils, diced potato (if using), vegetable broth, salt, pepper, paprika, cumin, and marjoram.
   o Bring to a boil, then reduce heat and simmer for 20-25 minutes until lentils and potatoes are soft.
3. **Blend the Soup (Optional):**

o   For a creamy consistency, use an immersion blender to partially or fully blend the soup.

4. **Finish & Serve:**
    o   Stir in the cream and let simmer for 2 more minutes.
    o   Garnish with fresh parsley and serve warm with crusty bread.

KRAUTSALAT (GERMAN COLESLAW)

Servings: 4

Ingredients:

- ½ head of white cabbage, finely shredded (about 500g / 1 lb)
- ½ small onion, finely chopped
- 1 small carrot, grated (optional)
- 1 tbsp salt (for softening the cabbage)

Dressing:

- 3 tbsp white vinegar
- 2 tbsp vegetable oil
- 1 tsp sugar
- ½ tsp salt
- ¼ tsp black pepper
- ½ tsp caraway seeds (optional, for authentic flavor)
- 1 tsp mustard (optional, for extra tang)

Instructions:

1. **Prepare the Cabbage:**
   o Place the shredded cabbage in a bowl, sprinkle with 1 tbsp salt, and massage it with your hands for about 2-3 minutes until it softens and releases liquid. Let sit for 10 minutes, then rinse and drain.
2. **Make the Dressing:**
   o In a small bowl, whisk together vinegar, oil, sugar, salt, pepper, caraway seeds, and mustard (if using).
3. **Assemble the Salad:**
   o In a large bowl, combine the cabbage, onion, and grated carrot (if using).
   o Pour the dressing over and toss well to coat.

4. **Chill & Serve:**
   o Let the salad sit in the fridge for at least 30 minutes (or up to a few hours) to allow the flavors to meld.

MAIN DISHES

KÄSESPÄTZLE (CHEESE SPAETZLE WITH CARAMELIZED ONIONS)

Servings: 4

Ingredients for the Spaetzle:

- 300g (2 ½ cups) all-purpose flour
- 1 tsp salt
- 3 eggs
- 120ml (½ cup) water or milk

Ingredients for the Cheese & Onions:

- 2 large onions, thinly sliced
- 2 tbsp butter
- 200g (2 cups) grated Emmental or Gruyère cheese (or a mix)

- ½ tsp salt
- ¼ tsp black pepper
- 1 tbsp chopped chives or parsley (for garnish)

Instructions:

Make the Spaetzle:

1. In a bowl, mix flour and salt. Add eggs and water (or milk), then stir until you get a thick, smooth batter. Let rest for 10 minutes.
2. Bring a large pot of salted water to a boil.
3. Using a spaetzle maker, colander, or cutting board, drop small amounts of batter into the boiling water. Cook until the spaetzle float to the top (about 2-3 minutes). Remove with a slotted spoon and set aside.

Caramelize the Onions:

4. In a pan, melt butter over low-medium heat. Add sliced onions and cook slowly for 15-20 minutes, stirring occasionally, until golden brown and soft.

Assemble the Dish:

5. Preheat oven to 180°C (350°F).
6. In a greased baking dish or pan, layer spaetzle and grated cheese, repeating until all ingredients are used.
7. Bake for 10-15 minutes, until the cheese is fully melted.

Serve:

8. Top with caramelized onions and garnish with chives or parsley.

VEGETARIAN MAULTASCHEN (GERMAN RAVIOLI)

Servings: 4 (Makes about 12 dumplings)

Ingredients for the Dough:

- 300g (2 ½ cups) all-purpose flour
- 2 eggs (or 4 tbsp water for vegan)
- 1 tbsp olive oil
- 1 pinch of salt
- 50ml (¼ cup) water (as needed)

Ingredients for the Filling:

- 200g (7 oz) spinach, cooked and chopped
- 100g (½ cup) ricotta or quark (use firm tofu for vegan)
- 1 small onion, finely chopped
- 1 clove garlic, minced
- 1 tbsp butter or olive oil
- 1 slice of bread, crumbled (or breadcrumbs)
- 1 tsp mustard
- ½ tsp salt
- ¼ tsp black pepper
- ½ tsp nutmeg

Instructions:

Make the Dough:

1. In a bowl, mix flour and salt. Add eggs, olive oil, and water as needed, kneading into a smooth dough.
2. Cover and let rest for 30 minutes.

Prepare the Filling:

3. Heat butter or oil in a pan. Sauté onions and garlic until soft.
4. In a bowl, mix cooked spinach, ricotta, breadcrumbs, mustard, salt, pepper, and nutmeg. Stir in the sautéed onions.

Assemble the Maultaschen:

5. Roll out the dough into a thin sheet (about 2mm thick). Cut into large rectangles (about 10x12 cm / 4x5 inches).
6. Place a spoonful of filling in the center of each rectangle. Fold the dough over and seal the edges with a bit of water, pressing firmly.

Cook the Maultaschen:

7. Bring a pot of salted water to a gentle boil. Drop the Maultaschen in and cook for 5-7 minutes until they float to the top.

Serve:

8. Drain and serve in a clear vegetable broth, pan-fried with butter and onions, or with a side of potato salad.

SCHUPFNUDELN WITH SAUERKRAUT (POTATO DUMPLINGS WITH SAUERKRAUT)

Servings: 4

Ingredients for the Schupfnudeln:

- 500g (1 lb) potatoes, boiled and peeled
- 150g (1 cup) all-purpose flour
- 1 egg (or 2 tbsp plant-based milk for vegan)
- ½ tsp salt
- ¼ tsp nutmeg

Ingredients for the Sauerkraut Mixture:

- 300g (2 cups) sauerkraut, drained
- 1 small onion, finely chopped
- 1 tbsp butter or oil
- ½ tsp caraway seeds (optional, for authentic flavor)
- ½ tsp sugar (optional, to balance acidity)
- Salt and black pepper, to taste

Instructions:

Make the Schupfnudeln:

1. Mash the boiled potatoes until smooth. Let cool.
2. In a bowl, mix mashed potatoes, flour, egg (or plant-based milk), salt, and nutmeg into a soft dough.
3. Lightly flour your hands and roll the dough into small logs, about finger-thick and 5 cm (2 inches) long.
4. Bring a pot of salted water to a gentle boil. Drop the dumplings in and cook until they float (about 3 minutes). Remove with a slotted spoon and let dry.

Prepare the Sauerkraut:

5. Heat butter or oil in a pan. Sauté onions until soft and golden.
6. Add sauerkraut, caraway seeds, sugar, salt, and black pepper. Cook for 5-10 minutes over low heat.

Crisp the Schupfnudeln & Serve:

7. In a separate pan, heat a little more butter or oil. Pan-fry the cooked Schupfnudeln until golden brown and crispy on the outside.
8. Add the sauerkraut mixture to the pan and toss everything together.

VEGETARIAN RINDERROULADEN (STUFFED CABBAGE ROLLS)

Servings: 4 (Makes 8 rolls)

Ingredients for the Cabbage Rolls:

- 8 large cabbage leaves
- 200g (7 oz) mushrooms, finely chopped
- 1 small onion, finely chopped
- 1 carrot, grated
- 1 small pickle, finely chopped
- 1 tbsp mustard
- 2 tbsp breadcrumbs
- 1 tbsp butter or olive oil
- ½ tsp salt
- ¼ tsp black pepper
- ½ tsp paprika

Ingredients for the Gravy:

- 1 tbsp butter or olive oil
- 1 tbsp all-purpose flour
- 500ml (2 cups) vegetable broth
- 1 tbsp tomato paste
- 1 tsp soy sauce (for umami)
- ½ tsp black pepper
- ½ tsp smoked paprika (optional)

Instructions:

Prepare the Cabbage Leaves:

1. Bring a pot of water to a boil. Blanch the cabbage leaves for 1-2 minutes until softened. Drain and set aside.

Make the Filling:

2. Heat butter or oil in a pan. Sauté onions, mushrooms, and carrots until soft (about 5 minutes).
3. Stir in mustard, chopped pickle, breadcrumbs, salt, pepper, and paprika. Remove from heat.

Assemble the Rolls:

4. Lay a cabbage leaf flat and place 1-2 tbsp of filling in the center.
5. Fold in the sides and roll up tightly. Secure with toothpicks or kitchen twine.

Make the Gravy & Cook the Rolls:

6. Heat butter or oil in a deep pan. Stir in flour and cook for 1 minute.
7. Add tomato paste, vegetable broth, soy sauce, black pepper, and smoked paprika. Stir until smooth.
8. Place cabbage rolls in the pan, cover, and simmer for 30 minutes, turning occasionally.

Serve:

9. Remove toothpicks or twine, spoon gravy over the rolls, and serve with mashed potatoes or dumplings.

PILZRAGOUT MIT SEMMELKNÖDEL (MUSHROOM RAGOUT WITH BREAD DUMPLINGS)

Servings: 4

Ingredients for the Semmelknödel (Bread Dumplings):

- 250g (5-6 cups) stale bread, cut into small cubes (white or sourdough)
- 250ml (1 cup) warm milk (or plant-based milk)
- 1 small onion, finely chopped
- 1 tbsp butter or olive oil
- 2 eggs (or 2 tbsp flaxseed mixed with 4 tbsp water for vegan)
- 2 tbsp fresh parsley, chopped
- ½ tsp salt
- ¼ tsp black pepper
- 2 tbsp breadcrumbs (if needed for binding)

Ingredients for the Pilzragout (Mushroom Ragout):

- 400g (14 oz) mixed mushrooms (button, cremini, or wild), sliced
- 1 small onion, finely chopped
- 1 clove garlic, minced
- 1 tbsp butter or olive oil
- 250ml (1 cup) vegetable broth
- 125ml (½ cup) heavy cream or plant-based cream
- 1 tbsp white wine or lemon juice (optional)
- ½ tsp salt
- ¼ tsp black pepper
- ½ tsp dried thyme or marjoram
- 1 tbsp fresh parsley, chopped (for garnish)

Instructions:

Make the Bread Dumplings:

1. In a large bowl, pour warm milk over the bread cubes and let soak for 10 minutes.
2. Meanwhile, sauté the onion in butter or oil until soft. Add to the bread mixture.
3. Stir in eggs, parsley, salt, and pepper. Mix well, adding breadcrumbs if the dough is too sticky.
4. Form into 4-6 round dumplings with damp hands.
5. Bring a large pot of salted water to a gentle simmer. Carefully drop in the dumplings and cook for 15-20 minutes until they float. Remove and set aside.

Make the Mushroom Ragout:

6. Heat butter or oil in a large pan over medium heat. Sauté onions and garlic for 2-3 minutes.
7. Add mushrooms, salt, pepper, and thyme. Cook for 5-7 minutes until soft.
8. Pour in vegetable broth and let simmer for 5 minutes.
9. Stir in cream and white wine or lemon juice (if using). Simmer for another 2 minutes. Adjust seasoning to taste.
10. Place dumplings on a plate, spoon mushroom ragout over the top, and garnish with fresh parsley.

GRÜNKOHL MIT PINKEL (KALE AND SMOKED VEGAN SAUSAGE)

Servings: 4

Ingredients:

- 500g (1 lb) fresh kale, washed and chopped (or 300g frozen kale)
- 1 tbsp butter or vegetable oil
- 1 small onion, finely chopped
- 2 cloves garlic, minced
- 500ml (2 cups) vegetable broth
- 2 medium potatoes, peeled and diced
- 2 tbsp rolled oats (helps thicken the dish)
- ½ tsp salt
- ¼ tsp black pepper
- ½ tsp mustard
- ½ tsp smoked paprika (optional, for a deeper flavor)
- 4 smoked vegan sausages (e.g., tofu or seitan-based)

Instructions:

1. **Prepare the Kale:**
   o If using fresh kale, blanch it in boiling water for 2 minutes, then drain.
2. **Sauté the Aromatics:**
   o Heat butter or oil in a large pot over medium heat.
   o Add the chopped onion and garlic, sautéing until soft and fragrant (about 3-4 minutes).
3. **Cook the Kale:**
   o Add the kale, vegetable broth, diced potatoes, rolled oats, salt, pepper, mustard, and smoked paprika.
   o Stir well, cover, and let simmer for 30-40 minutes, stirring occasionally.

GERMAN VEGETARIAN COOKBOOK

4. **Cook the Vegan Sausages:**
   - o In a separate pan, lightly fry the vegan sausages until browned and heated through.

5. **Serve:**
   - o Spoon the kale and potatoes onto a plate and place the smoked sausages on top.
   - o Serve with mustard and rustic bread or boiled potatoes on the side.

VEGETARIAN GULASCH (GERMAN GOULASH WITH MUSHROOMS & PEPPERS)

Servings: 4

Ingredients:

- 2 tbsp olive oil
- 1 large onion, chopped
- 2 cloves garlic, minced
- 400g (14 oz) mushrooms, sliced (button, cremini, or mixed)
- 2 bell peppers (red and yellow), chopped
- 2 medium potatoes, peeled and diced (optional, for extra heartiness)
- 1 tbsp tomato paste
- 1 tsp sweet paprika
- ½ tsp smoked paprika
- ½ tsp caraway seeds (optional, for authentic flavor)
- 500ml (2 cups) vegetable broth
- 1 tbsp soy sauce (adds umami)
- 1 tsp apple cider vinegar or red wine vinegar
- ½ tsp salt
- ¼ tsp black pepper
- 1 tbsp cornstarch mixed with 2 tbsp water (optional, for thickening)
- Fresh parsley, chopped (for garnish)

Instructions:

1. **Sauté the Aromatics:**
   - Heat olive oil in a large pot over medium heat.
   - Add onions and garlic, sautéing until soft (about 3-4 minutes).
2. **Cook the Vegetables:**

- o Add mushrooms and bell peppers. Cook for 5-7 minutes until softened.
- o Stir in tomato paste, sweet and smoked paprika, and caraway seeds (if using). Cook for another minute to enhance the flavors.

3. **Simmer the Gulasch:**
   - o Pour in vegetable broth, soy sauce, vinegar, potatoes (if using), salt, and black pepper. Stir well.
   - o Bring to a gentle simmer, cover, and cook for 20-25 minutes until the vegetables are tender.

4. **Thicken the Sauce (Optional):**
   - o If a thicker consistency is desired, mix cornstarch with water and stir into the goulash. Simmer for another 2 minutes.

5. **Serve:**
   - o Garnish with fresh parsley and serve hot with bread, spaetzle, or dumplings.

RAHMSCHWAMMERL MIT KNÖDELN (CREAMY MUSHROOM STEW WITH DUMPLINGS)

Servings: 4

Ingredients for the Mushroom Stew:

- 2 tbsp butter or olive oil
- 1 small onion, finely chopped
- 2 cloves garlic, minced
- 400g (14 oz) mixed mushrooms (button, cremini, or wild), sliced
- 1 tbsp all-purpose flour (for thickening)
- 250ml (1 cup) vegetable broth
- 125ml (½ cup) heavy cream or plant-based cream
- 1 tsp lemon juice
- ½ tsp salt
- ¼ tsp black pepper
- ½ tsp dried thyme or marjoram
- 1 tbsp fresh parsley, chopped (for garnish)

Ingredients for the Semmelknödel (Bread Dumplings):

- 250g (5-6 cups) stale bread, cut into small cubes (white or sourdough)
- 250ml (1 cup) warm milk (or plant-based milk)
- 1 small onion, finely chopped
- 1 tbsp butter or olive oil
- 2 eggs (or 2 tbsp flaxseed mixed with 4 tbsp water for vegan)
- 2 tbsp fresh parsley, chopped
- ½ tsp salt
- ¼ tsp black pepper
- 2 tbsp breadcrumbs (if needed for binding)

Instructions:

Make the Bread Dumplings:

1. In a large bowl, pour warm milk over the bread cubes and let soak for 10 minutes.
2. Meanwhile, sauté the onion in butter or oil until soft. Add to the bread mixture.
3. Stir in eggs, parsley, salt, and pepper. Mix well, adding breadcrumbs if the dough is too sticky.
4. Form into 4-6 round dumplings with damp hands.
5. Bring a large pot of salted water to a gentle simmer. Carefully drop in the dumplings and cook for 15-20 minutes until they float. Remove and set aside.

Make the Mushroom Stew:

6. Heat butter or oil in a large pan over medium heat. Sauté onions and garlic for 2-3 minutes.
7. Add mushrooms, salt, pepper, and thyme. Cook for 5-7 minutes until mushrooms release their juices.
8. Sprinkle in flour, stir well, and cook for 1 minute.
9. Pour in vegetable broth and let simmer for 5 minutes.
10. Stir in cream and lemon juice. Simmer for another 2 minutes. Adjust seasoning to taste.

Serve:

11. Place dumplings on a plate, spoon creamy mushroom stew over the top, and garnish with fresh parsley.

ROTKOHL (GERMAN RED CABBAGE)

Servings: 4

Ingredients:

- 1 small head of red cabbage, finely shredded
- 1 medium onion, finely chopped
- 1 tbsp butter or olive oil
- 1 apple, peeled and grated (or finely chopped)
- 2 tbsp apple cider vinegar
- 1 tbsp sugar (or maple syrup for a vegan option)
- 1 tsp salt
- ¼ tsp black pepper
- ½ tsp ground cloves
- ½ tsp ground cinnamon
- 1 bay leaf

- 250ml (1 cup) vegetable broth
- 1 tbsp fresh parsley, chopped (for garnish)

Instructions:

1. **Sauté the Onion & Apple:**
   o Heat butter or oil in a large pot over medium heat.
   o Add the onion and cook for 3-4 minutes until softened.
   o Stir in the grated apple and cook for another 2 minutes.
2. **Cook the Cabbage:**
   o Add the shredded red cabbage to the pot and stir well.
   o Pour in the apple cider vinegar, sugar, salt, pepper, cloves, cinnamon, and bay leaf.
   o Mix to combine, then add vegetable broth. Bring to a simmer.
3. **Simmer:**
   o Cover and cook on low heat for 40-45 minutes, stirring occasionally, until the cabbage is tender and the flavors have melded.
4. **Finish & Serve:**
   o Remove the bay leaf, adjust seasoning if needed, and garnish with fresh parsley.

SPECKKARTOFFELSALAT (BAVARIAN POTATO SALAD)

Servings: 4

Ingredients:

- 800g (1 ¾ lbs) waxy potatoes, peeled and boiled
- 1 small onion, finely chopped
- 2 tbsp vegetable oil
- 2 tbsp apple cider vinegar
- 1 tbsp Dijon mustard
- 1 tsp sugar
- 1 tsp salt
- ¼ tsp black pepper
- 100g (3.5 oz) smoked vegan bacon or plant-based sausage, chopped (or regular bacon if not vegetarian)
- 1 tbsp fresh parsley, chopped (for garnish)

Instructions:

1. **Prepare the Potatoes:**
   o Boil the potatoes in salted water until tender (about 15-20 minutes). Drain, let cool slightly, and slice them into 1 cm (½ inch) thick slices.
2. **Make the Dressing:**
   o In a small bowl, whisk together vegetable oil, apple cider vinegar, Dijon mustard, sugar, salt, and pepper. Set aside.
3. **Cook the Vegan Bacon (or Regular Bacon):**
   o In a pan, heat a little oil over medium heat. Add the chopped vegan bacon (or regular bacon) and cook until crispy, about 5-7 minutes.
4. **Assemble the Salad:**

- o In a large bowl, gently toss the warm potatoes with the chopped onions, crispy bacon, and mustard dressing.
- o Mix carefully so the potatoes don't break apart.

5. **Serve:**
   - o Let the salad sit for about 20 minutes to allow the flavors to blend. Garnish with fresh parsley before serving.

DILL-GURKENSALAT (DILL CUCUMBER SALAD)

Servings: 4

Ingredients:

- 2 medium cucumbers, thinly sliced
- ½ small onion, finely sliced
- 1 tbsp salt
- 150ml (½ cup) plain yogurt or plant-based yogurt (for vegan)
- 2 tbsp white wine vinegar
- 1 tbsp olive oil
- 1 tsp sugar
- 1 tsp fresh dill, chopped (or ½ tsp dried dill)
- ¼ tsp black pepper

Instructions:

1. **Prepare the Cucumbers:**
   o Place the sliced cucumbers in a bowl and sprinkle with salt.
   o Let sit for 10-15 minutes to release excess moisture, then gently pat dry with paper towels.
2. **Make the Dressing:**
   o In a small bowl, whisk together yogurt, vinegar, olive oil, sugar, dill, and black pepper until smooth.
3. **Assemble the Salad:**
   o Add the cucumber slices and onion to the bowl with the dressing. Toss to combine.
4. **Serve:**
   o Chill in the fridge for 15-20 minutes to allow the flavors to meld. Serve fresh and cool.

BRATKARTOFFELN (GERMAN FRIED POTATOES)

Servings: 4

Ingredients:

- 800g (1 ¾ lbs) waxy potatoes, peeled and cut into thin slices
- 2 tbsp vegetable oil or butter
- 1 medium onion, thinly sliced
- 1 clove garlic, minced (optional)
- 1 tsp dried thyme or rosemary
- ½ tsp salt
- ¼ tsp black pepper
- Fresh parsley, chopped (for garnish)

Instructions:

1. **Prepare the Potatoes:**
   o Boil the potatoes in salted water for 10-12 minutes, until just tender but not falling apart. Drain and let cool slightly. Slice the potatoes into 1 cm (½ inch) thick rounds.
2. **Fry the Potatoes:**
   o Heat oil or butter in a large skillet over medium heat. Add the sliced potatoes and fry, turning occasionally, until golden and crispy (about 10-12 minutes).
3. **Sauté the Onions:**
   o While the potatoes are frying, sauté the sliced onions in a separate pan with a little oil or butter for 5-7 minutes until softened and slightly caramelized. Add garlic during the last minute if using.
4. **Combine & Season:**

- o Once the potatoes are crispy, stir in the sautéed onions. Sprinkle with thyme or rosemary, salt, and pepper. Toss gently to combine.

5. **Serve:**
   - o Garnish with fresh parsley and serve warm.

BLAUKRAUT (SWEET AND SOUR RED CABBAGE)

Servings: 4

Ingredients:

- 1 small head of red cabbage, finely shredded
- 1 small onion, finely chopped
- 1 tbsp butter or olive oil
- 2 tbsp apple cider vinegar
- 2 tbsp sugar (or maple syrup for a vegan option)
- ½ tsp salt
- ¼ tsp black pepper
- 1 tsp ground cinnamon
- 2-3 whole cloves (or ½ tsp ground cloves)
- 250ml (1 cup) vegetable broth
- 1 bay leaf
- 1 apple, peeled and grated or chopped (optional, for extra sweetness)

Instructions:

1. **Sauté the Onion:**
   - In a large pot, heat butter or olive oil over medium heat.
   - Add the chopped onion and cook for 3-4 minutes until softened.
2. **Cook the Cabbage:**
   - Add the shredded cabbage to the pot and stir well.
   - Pour in apple cider vinegar, sugar, salt, pepper, cinnamon, cloves, and vegetable broth. Stir to combine.
3. **Simmer the Cabbage:**
   - Add the bay leaf and grated apple (if using).

- o Bring the mixture to a boil, then reduce the heat and simmer, uncovered, for 40-45 minutes, stirring occasionally, until the cabbage is tender and the flavors are well blended.

4. **Finish & Serve:**
   - o Remove the bay leaf and adjust seasoning if necessary.
   - o Serve warm as a side dish to your favorite German main course.

SAUERKRAUT MIT APFEL (SAUERKRAUT WITH APPLE & CARAWAY)

Servings: 4

Ingredients:

- 500g (2 cups) sauerkraut, drained
- 1 medium apple, peeled, cored, and chopped
- 1 small onion, finely chopped
- 1 tbsp butter or olive oil
- 1 tsp caraway seeds
- 1 tbsp apple cider vinegar
- 1 tbsp sugar or maple syrup (optional, for extra sweetness)
- ½ tsp salt
- ¼ tsp black pepper
- 250ml (1 cup) vegetable broth
- 1 bay leaf

Instructions:

1. **Sauté the Onion and Apple:**
   - Heat butter or oil in a large pan over medium heat.
   - Add the chopped onion and cook for 3-4 minutes until softened.
   - Stir in the apple and cook for another 3-4 minutes until the apple begins to soften.
2. **Cook the Sauerkraut:**
   - Add the sauerkraut to the pan along with caraway seeds, apple cider vinegar, sugar (if using), salt, pepper, and vegetable broth.
   - Stir to combine and bring to a simmer.
3. **Simmer:**

- o Add the bay leaf and cook the sauerkraut mixture on low heat for 25-30 minutes, stirring occasionally, until the flavors have melded together and the cabbage is tender.

4. **Finish & Serve:**
   - o Remove the bay leaf and adjust seasoning if needed. Serve warm alongside your favorite German mains, like sausages or schnitzel.

KARTOFFELKLÖSSE (GERMAN POTATO DUMPLINGS)

Servings: 4 (Makes 8-10 dumplings)

Ingredients:

- 1 kg (2.2 lbs) waxy potatoes (e.g., Yukon Gold), peeled and boiled
- 150g (1 cup) all-purpose flour
- 2 tbsp potato starch (optional, for extra fluffiness)
- 1 large egg
- ½ tsp salt
- ¼ tsp nutmeg (optional)
- 2 tbsp butter, melted
- 1 tbsp fresh parsley, chopped (optional, for garnish)

Instructions:

1. **Prepare the Potatoes:**
   - Boil the potatoes in salted water until tender, about 20 minutes. Drain and let cool slightly.
   - Mash the potatoes until smooth, making sure there are no lumps. Let them cool completely.
2. **Make the Dough:**
   - Once the potatoes are cool, mix in the flour, potato starch (if using), egg, salt, and nutmeg. Stir until you form a smooth dough. If the dough is too sticky, add a little more flour.
3. **Shape the Dumplings:**
   - With damp hands, divide the dough into 8-10 portions and shape each portion into a ball. Make a small indentation in the center of each ball (you can fill it with a small piece of butter for extra flavor, if desired).
4. **Cook the Dumplings:**

- o   Bring a large pot of salted water to a gentle simmer. Carefully drop the dumplings into the water. Cook for 15-20 minutes until they float to the surface.

5. **Serve:**
   - o   Remove the dumplings with a slotted spoon. Drizzle with melted butter and sprinkle with fresh parsley.

SPARGEL MIT HOLLANDAISE (WHITE ASPARAGUS WITH HOLLANDAISE SAUCE)

Servings: 4

Ingredients for the Asparagus:

- 1 kg (2.2 lbs) white asparagus, peeled and trimmed
- 1 tbsp sugar
- 1 tbsp salt
- 1 tbsp butter (optional, for serving)

Ingredients for the Hollandaise Sauce:

- 3 large egg yolks
- 200g (7 oz) unsalted butter, melted
- 1 tbsp lemon juice
- 1 tsp Dijon mustard (optional)
- ¼ tsp salt
- ¼ tsp white pepper (optional)

Instructions:

Prepare the Asparagus:

1. **Peel and Trim the Asparagus:**
   o Peel the white asparagus carefully, removing any tough, fibrous skin. Cut off the woody ends.
2. **Cook the Asparagus:**
   o Bring a large pot of salted water to a boil. Add the sugar and salt, then carefully add the asparagus.
   o Simmer gently for about 10-15 minutes, depending on the thickness of the asparagus, until tender but still firm. Drain and set aside.

Make the Hollandaise Sauce:

3. **Prepare the Sauce:**
   o In a heatproof bowl, whisk the egg yolks with the lemon juice, salt, and mustard (if using).
4. **Cook the Sauce:**
   o In a saucepan, melt the butter over low heat. Slowly pour the warm melted butter into the egg yolks while whisking continuously until the sauce thickens to a creamy consistency. If the sauce is too thick, you can thin it with a little warm water.
   o Taste and adjust seasoning with salt, pepper, and more lemon juice if needed.
   o Arrange the cooked asparagus on serving plates, drizzle with hollandaise sauce, and top with a pat of butter if desired.

VOLLKORNBROT (TRADITIONAL GERMAN WHOLE GRAIN BREAD)

Servings: 12 slices

Ingredients:

- 300g (2 ½ cups) whole wheat flour
- 200g (1 ½ cups) rye flour
- 1 packet (7g / 2 ¼ tsp) active dry yeast
- 1 ½ tsp salt
- 1 tsp sugar
- 350ml (1 ½ cups) warm water
- 2 tbsp vegetable oil or melted butter
- 1 tbsp apple cider vinegar
- 100g (½ cup) sunflower seeds or mixed seeds (optional, for extra texture)

Instructions:

1. **Prepare the Yeast Mixture:**
   o In a small bowl, combine warm water, sugar, and yeast. Stir and let sit for 5-10 minutes until the yeast becomes frothy.

2. **Make the Dough:**
   o In a large mixing bowl, combine the whole wheat flour, rye flour, and salt. Add the yeast mixture, vegetable oil (or melted butter), and apple cider vinegar.
   o Stir to form a sticky dough. If the dough is too dry, add a little more water, 1 tablespoon at a time.

3. **Knead the Dough:**
   o Turn the dough out onto a lightly floured surface and knead for about 8-10 minutes until smooth and elastic.
   o If using, gently fold in the sunflower seeds or mixed seeds.

4. **Let the Dough Rise:**
   o Place the dough in a lightly oiled bowl, cover with a clean towel, and let it rise in a warm place for 1-1.5 hours, or until doubled in size.

5. **Shape the Loaf:**
   o Preheat the oven to 200°C (400°F).
   o Punch down the dough and shape it into a loaf. Place the dough in a greased or parchment-lined loaf pan.

6. **Bake the Bread:**
   o Bake for 30-35 minutes, or until the bread sounds hollow when tapped on the bottom.
   o Let the bread cool on a wire rack before slicing.

ROGGENBROT (GERMAN RYE BREAD)

Servings: 12 slices

Ingredients:

- 400g (3 ½ cups) rye flour
- 100g (¾ cup) all-purpose flour
- 1 packet (7g / 2 ¼ tsp) active dry yeast
- 1 ½ tsp salt
- 1 tsp caraway seeds (optional, for authentic flavor)
- 1 tsp sugar
- 350ml (1 ½ cups) warm water
- 2 tbsp vegetable oil or melted butter
- 1 tbsp apple cider vinegar
- 1 tbsp honey (optional, for a hint of sweetness)

Instructions:

1. **Activate the Yeast:**
   - In a small bowl, combine warm water, sugar, and yeast. Stir and let sit for 5-10 minutes until it becomes frothy.
2. **Mix the Dough:**
   - In a large mixing bowl, combine rye flour, all-purpose flour, salt, and caraway seeds (if using).
   - Add the yeast mixture, vegetable oil (or melted butter), apple cider vinegar, and honey (if using).
   - Stir until you form a sticky dough.
3. **Knead the Dough:**
   - Turn the dough onto a floured surface and knead for about 8-10 minutes, adding flour as necessary to prevent sticking. The dough should be dense and firm.
4. **Let the Dough Rise:**

- o Place the dough in a lightly greased bowl and cover with a damp towel. Let it rise in a warm place for 1-1.5 hours or until it has doubled in size.

5. **Shape the Loaf:**
   - o Preheat the oven to 220°C (425°F).
   - o Punch down the dough and shape it into a round or oval loaf. Place it on a greased or parchment-lined baking sheet.

6. **Bake the Bread:**
   - o Bake the loaf for 30-40 minutes, or until it sounds hollow when tapped on the bottom.
   - o If you prefer a darker crust, you can lightly spray the oven with water 5 minutes before baking ends.

7. **Cool and Serve:**
   - o Let the bread cool on a wire rack before slicing.

BREZELN (AUTHENTIC GERMAN PRETZELS)

Servings: 8 pretzels

Ingredients:

- 500g (4 cups) all-purpose flour
- 1 packet (7g / 2 ¼ tsp) active dry yeast
- 1 tsp salt
- 1 tsp sugar
- 300ml (1 ¼ cups) warm water
- 2 tbsp butter, melted
- 1 tbsp baking soda (for the boiling bath)
- Coarse salt (for topping)

Instructions:

1. **Prepare the Dough:**
   - In a small bowl, combine warm water, sugar, and yeast. Stir and let sit for 5-10 minutes until the yeast becomes frothy.
   - In a large mixing bowl, combine flour and salt. Add the yeast mixture and melted butter, and stir until a dough forms.
   - Knead the dough for about 10 minutes until it becomes smooth and elastic. If the dough is too sticky, add a little more flour.
2. **Let the Dough Rise:**
   - Cover the dough with a damp towel or plastic wrap and let it rise in a warm place for 1 hour or until doubled in size.
3. **Shape the Pretzels:**
   - Preheat your oven to 220°C (425°F).

63

o Punch down the dough and divide it into 8 equal pieces.

o Roll each piece into a long rope (about 50 cm / 20 inches long) and form into a pretzel shape by crossing the ends and twisting them into a knot.

4. **Boil the Pretzels:**

o Bring a large pot of water to a boil and add the baking soda.

o Gently drop each pretzel into the boiling water for about 30 seconds. Use a slotted spoon to remove them and place them on a parchment-lined baking sheet.

5. **Bake the Pretzels:**

o Sprinkle the pretzels with coarse salt and bake for 12-15 minutes, or until golden brown and crispy.

6. **Cool and Serve:**

o Allow the pretzels to cool slightly before serving with mustard, cheese, or your favorite dipping sauce.

KARTOFFELBROT (GERMAN POTATO BREAD)

Servings: 12 slices

Ingredients:

- 500g (4 cups) all-purpose flour
- 250g (1 ½ cups) mashed potatoes (about 2 medium potatoes)
- 1 packet (7g / 2 ¼ tsp) active dry yeast
- 1 tsp salt
- 1 tsp sugar
- 300ml (1 ¼ cups) warm water
- 2 tbsp vegetable oil or melted butter
- 1 tbsp apple cider vinegar (optional, for tanginess)

Instructions:

1. **Prepare the Yeast Mixture:**
   - In a small bowl, combine warm water, sugar, and yeast. Stir and let sit for 5-10 minutes until it becomes frothy.
2. **Make the Dough:**
   - In a large mixing bowl, combine the mashed potatoes, flour, and salt.
   - Add the yeast mixture, vegetable oil (or melted butter), and apple cider vinegar (if using).
   - Stir everything together until a dough forms. If the dough feels too sticky, add a little more flour.
3. **Knead the Dough:**
   - Turn the dough out onto a lightly floured surface and knead for about 8-10 minutes until it becomes smooth and elastic.
   - If using a stand mixer, knead with the dough hook for about 5-6 minutes.

4. **Let the Dough Rise:**
   - o   Place the dough in a lightly oiled bowl, cover with a damp towel or plastic wrap, and let it rise in a warm place for about 1-1.5 hours or until doubled in size.

5. **Shape the Loaf:**
   - o   Preheat the oven to 220°C (425°F).
   - o   Punch down the dough and shape it into a round or oval loaf. Place it on a greased or parchment-lined baking sheet.

6. **Bake the Bread:**
   - o   Bake the bread for 25-30 minutes, or until it sounds hollow when tapped on the bottom.
   - o   Let the bread cool on a wire rack before slicing.

ZWETSCHGENKUCHEN (GERMAN PLUM CAKE)

Servings: 8-10

Ingredients for the Cake Dough:

- 250g (2 cups) all-purpose flour
- 125g (½ cup) unsalted butter, softened
- 100g (½ cup) sugar
- 1 large egg
- 1 tsp vanilla extract
- 1 tsp baking powder
- ½ tsp salt
- 50ml (¼ cup) milk

Ingredients for the Plum Topping:

- 500g (1 lb) fresh plums, pitted and sliced
- 1 tbsp sugar (optional, depending on the sweetness of the plums)
- 1 tsp ground cinnamon (optional, for extra flavor)

Ingredients for the Streusel (Crumble Topping):

- 100g (½ cup) all-purpose flour
- 50g (¼ cup) sugar
- 50g (¼ cup) unsalted butter, cold and cubed

Instructions:

Prepare the Cake Dough:

1. **Preheat the Oven:**

    o Preheat the oven to 180°C (350°F). Grease and flour a 9-inch (23 cm) springform pan or line it with parchment paper.

2. **Make the Dough:**
   - o In a large mixing bowl, beat the softened butter and sugar until light and creamy.
   - o Add the egg, vanilla extract, baking powder, salt, and milk. Mix until smooth.
   - o Gradually add the flour and mix until you have a soft dough.

Assemble the Cake:

3. **Prepare the Plums:**
   - o Slice the plums into halves or quarters, removing the pits. If desired, sprinkle with a little sugar and cinnamon to enhance their sweetness.
4. **Spread the Dough:**
   - o Press the dough into the prepared pan, spreading it evenly across the bottom.
5. **Arrange the Plums:**
   - o Arrange the sliced plums in a circular pattern over the dough, overlapping slightly.

Make the Streusel (Crumble Topping):

6. **Prepare the Streusel:**
   - o In a small bowl, combine flour, sugar, and cubed cold butter. Use your fingers or a pastry cutter to rub the butter into the dry ingredients until the mixture resembles coarse crumbs.
7. **Add the Streusel:**
   - o Sprinkle the streusel evenly over the plums.

Bake the Cake:

8. **Bake the Cake:**
    o Bake in the preheated oven for 40-45 minutes, or until the cake is golden brown and a toothpick inserted into the center comes out clean.

Serve:

9. **Cool and Serve:**
    o Let the cake cool slightly before slicing. Enjoy warm or at room temperature, optionally dusted with powdered sugar.

APFELSTRUDEL (CLASSIC APPLE STRUDEL)

Servings: 8

Ingredients for the Strudel Filling:

- 6 medium apples (preferably tart apples like Granny Smith), peeled, cored, and sliced
- 100g (½ cup) sugar
- 1 tsp ground cinnamon
- 1 tbsp lemon juice
- 50g (¼ cup) raisins (optional)
- 50g (¼ cup) breadcrumbs
- 2 tbsp unsalted butter, melted
- 1 tbsp vanilla extract

Ingredients for the Dough:

- 250g (2 cups) all-purpose flour
- 1 tbsp sugar
- ¼ tsp salt
- 1 large egg
- 2 tbsp vegetable oil
- 120ml (½ cup) warm water
- 2 tbsp melted butter (for brushing)

Instructions:

Make the Strudel Dough:

1. **Mix the Dough:**
   - In a large mixing bowl, combine the flour, sugar, and salt.
   - Add the egg, oil, and warm water. Mix to form a soft dough.
2. **Knead the Dough:**

o Turn the dough out onto a floured surface and knead for about 5-7 minutes until smooth and elastic.

3. **Let the Dough Rest:**
   o Place the dough in a bowl, cover it with a damp towel or plastic wrap, and let it rest for at least 30 minutes.

Prepare the Apple Filling:

4. **Prepare the Apples:**
   o While the dough is resting, mix the sliced apples with sugar, cinnamon, lemon juice, raisins (if using), and vanilla extract. Stir until well combined.

5. **Toast the Breadcrumbs:**
   o In a small pan, melt the butter over medium heat and add the breadcrumbs. Cook, stirring frequently, until the breadcrumbs are golden and crispy. Set aside.

Assemble the Strudel:

6. **Roll Out the Dough:**
   o After the dough has rested, place it on a large clean kitchen towel or a well-floured surface. Using a rolling pin, gently roll the dough out into a large, thin rectangle, about 16x12 inches (40x30 cm). The dough should be very thin, almost translucent.

7. **Add the Filling:**
   o Brush the rolled-out dough with melted butter. Sprinkle the toasted breadcrumbs evenly over the dough, leaving about 1 inch (2.5 cm) along the edges.
   o Layer the apple mixture evenly on top of the breadcrumbs.

8. **Roll the Strudel:**
   o Carefully roll up the dough, starting from one long edge, using the towel to help you roll it tightly. Pinch the edges to seal the strudel.

Bake the Apfelstrudel:

9. **Prepare for Baking:**
   o   Preheat your oven to 180°C (350°F).
   o   Transfer the rolled strudel onto a parchment-lined baking sheet. Brush the top with melted butter.
10. **Bake the Strudel:**

- Bake for 35-40 minutes, or until the strudel is golden brown and crisp. Halfway through baking, brush the top with more melted butter to enhance the golden crust.
- Let the strudel cool for a few minutes before slicing. Serve warm, dusted with powdered sugar if desired.

MOHNKUCHEN (POPPY SEED CAKE)

Servings: 8-10

Ingredients for the Cake:

- 200g (1 ½ cups) all-purpose flour
- 1 tsp baking powder
- 100g (½ cup) sugar
- 1 tsp vanilla extract
- 2 large eggs
- 150g (2/3 cup) unsalted butter, melted
- 100ml (½ cup) milk

Ingredients for the Poppy Seed Filling:

- 200g (1 ½ cups) ground poppy seeds
- 150ml (2/3 cup) milk
- 100g (½ cup) sugar
- 1 tbsp honey (optional)
- 1 tsp vanilla extract
- 1 tbsp lemon juice (optional, for extra freshness)

Ingredients for the Glaze:

- 100g (½ cup) powdered sugar
- 2 tbsp lemon juice (or water, for a milder glaze)

Instructions:

Make the Cake:

1. **Preheat the Oven:**
   - Preheat your oven to 180°C (350°F). Grease and flour a round or square cake pan (about 9 inches/23 cm).

2. **Mix the Dry Ingredients:**
   - o In a bowl, whisk together flour, baking powder, and sugar.
3. **Combine the Wet Ingredients:**
   - o In another bowl, whisk the eggs, melted butter, milk, and vanilla extract together.
4. **Make the Cake Batter:**
   - o Pour the wet ingredients into the dry ingredients and mix until smooth.
5. **Bake the Cake:**
   - o Pour the batter into the prepared pan and bake for 20-25 minutes, or until a toothpick inserted in the center comes out clean. Allow the cake to cool in the pan for 10 minutes, then remove and let it cool completely on a wire rack.

Prepare the Poppy Seed Filling:

6. **Cook the Poppy Seed Filling:**
   - o In a small saucepan, combine the ground poppy seeds, milk, sugar, honey (if using), vanilla extract, and lemon juice.
   - o Heat over medium-low, stirring frequently, until the mixture thickens and becomes a paste (about 5-7 minutes). Remove from heat and let cool.

Assemble the Cake:

7. **Spread the Filling:**
   - o Once the cake has cooled, slice it horizontally into two layers. Spread the cooled poppy seed filling evenly on the bottom layer.
8. **Top the Cake:**
   - o Place the second cake layer on top and gently press down.

Make the Glaze:

9. **Prepare the Glaze:**
   - In a small bowl, mix the powdered sugar and lemon juice (or water) to form a smooth glaze.

10. **Glaze the Cake:**

- Drizzle the glaze over the top of the cake, letting it run down the sides.
- Allow the glaze to set before slicing and serving.

BIENENSTICH (BEE STING CAKE WITH ALMOND & CUSTARD FILLING)

Servings: 8-10

Ingredients for the Dough:

- 250g (2 cups) all-purpose flour
- 1 packet (7g / 2 ¼ tsp) active dry yeast
- 1 tsp sugar
- 1 tsp salt
- 150ml (2/3 cup) warm milk
- 50g (¼ cup) unsalted butter, softened
- 1 large egg

Ingredients for the Almond Topping:

- 100g (½ cup) sliced almonds
- 100g (½ cup) sugar
- 50g (¼ cup) unsalted butter
- 2 tbsp honey

Ingredients for the Custard Filling:

- 250ml (1 cup) whole milk
- 2 large egg yolks
- 50g (¼ cup) sugar
- 1 tbsp cornstarch
- 1 tsp vanilla extract
- 100g (½ cup) unsalted butter, softened

Instructions:

Make the Dough:

1. **Activate the Yeast:**
   - In a small bowl, combine the warm milk, sugar, and yeast. Let it sit for about 5-10 minutes, until frothy.
2. **Prepare the Dough:**
   - In a large bowl, combine the flour and salt. Add the yeast mixture, softened butter, and egg. Mix until you form a smooth dough.
3. **Let the Dough Rise:**
   - Cover the bowl with a clean kitchen towel and let the dough rise in a warm place for about 1 hour, or until doubled in size.
4. **Shape and Preheat the Oven:**
   - Preheat your oven to 180°C (350°F). Grease and line a round cake pan (about 9 inches / 23 cm).
   - Punch down the dough and press it into the prepared cake pan, making sure it's evenly spread.

Prepare the Almond Topping:

5. **Make the Topping:**
   - In a small saucepan, melt the butter, sugar, and honey over medium heat. Stir until smooth and the sugar dissolves.
6. **Add the Almonds:**
   - Remove from heat and stir in the sliced almonds until they're evenly coated.
7. **Add the Topping to the Dough:**
   - Spread the almond mixture evenly over the risen dough in the cake pan.

Bake the Cake:

8. **Bake the Cake:**
   - Bake for 25-30 minutes, or until the cake is golden brown and the almond topping is caramelized. Let it cool completely in the pan.

Make the Custard Filling:

9. **Prepare the Custard:**
    o   In a saucepan, heat the milk over medium heat until it just begins to steam (but not boil).
    o   In a separate bowl, whisk together the egg yolks, sugar, and cornstarch. Slowly pour the hot milk into the egg mixture, whisking constantly.
    o   Return the mixture to the saucepan and cook over low heat, stirring constantly, until the custard thickens. Remove from heat and stir in the vanilla extract. Let it cool slightly.

10. **Add the Butter:**

- Stir in the softened butter until the custard is smooth and well-combined. Let the custard cool completely.

Assemble the Cake:

11. **Fill the Cake:**

- Once the cake has cooled, carefully slice it horizontally into two layers.
- Spread the cooled custard filling evenly over the bottom layer of the cake. Place the almond-topped layer on top.
- Let the cake set for about 30 minutes before slicing to allow the custard to firm up.

MEASUREMENT CONVERSIONS

LIQUID MEASUREMENTS

Metric	US Customary
1 liter (L)	4.2 cups
500 ml	2 cups
250 ml	1 cup
125 ml	1/2 cup
60 ml	1/4 cup
15 ml	1 tablespoon (tbsp)
5 ml	1 teaspoon (tsp)

TEMPERATURE CONVERSIONS

Celsius	Fahrenheit
100°C	212°F (boiling)
190°C	375°F
180°C	350°F
160°C	320°F
120°C	250°F

.

Printed by Amazon Italia Logistica S.r.l.
Torrazza Piemonte (TO), Italy